PROPHETIC BRIDGES

Discovering God's Pathways to Your Destiny!

by David Mayorga

Published by

SHABAR PUBLICATIONS
www.shabarpublications.com

Prophetic Bridges

Most Shabar Publications products are available at special quantity discounts for bulk purchase for sales promotions, fund-raising and educational needs. For details, write Shabar Publications at mayorga1126@gmail.com.

Prophetic Bridges: Discovering God's Pathways to Your Destiny
by David Mayorga
Published by Shabar Publications
3833 N. Taylor Rd.
Palmhurst, Texas 78573
www.shabarpublications.com
www.masterbuildertx.com

This book or parts thereof may not be reproduced in any form, stored in a retrieval system, or transmitted in any form by any means - electronic, mechanical, photocopy, recording, or otherwise - without prior written permission of the publisher, except as provided by United States of America copyright law.

Unless otherwise noted, all Scripture quotations are from the New Kings James Version of the Bible. Copyright@1979, 1980, 1982 by Thomas Nelson, Inc., publishers. Used by permission.

Edited by Adele Beltrán

Copyright @ 2021 by David Mayorga
All rights reserved

ISBN 978-1-7333174-5-0

David Mayorga

Discovering God's Pathways to Your Destiny

Content

Foreword 5

Preface 8

Introduction: Bridges - Where Did the Idea Come From? .. 12

Chapter 1: Prophetic Bridges are More than a
Pathways - They are an Opportunity 17

Chapter 2: Understanding Where You are Now 29

Chapter 3: Abraham: A Bridge for the Making of a Nation   40

Chapter 4: Noah: God's Bridge-Builder for Generations
Yet to be Born! 48

Chapter 5: Joshua: Making a Bridge to Conquer
the Impossible!. 57

Chapter 6: Peter: A Bridge to Cross Over 64

David Mayorga

Prophetic Bridges

Chapter 7: Saul of Tarsus: "Indeed, I Myself Thought . . . " 78

Chapter 8: John the Revelator: A Bridge to the Future 84

Chapter 9: Invitations, Methods and What Is Left Behind . . 92

Chapter 10: It's Now or Never! 103

Ministry Information 109

Ministry Resources 110

David Mayorga

Discovering God's Pathways to Your Destiny

Foreword

I have known David Mayorga for over twenty years now, as a colleague in the ministry, and as a personal friend. Throughout the years, he has been a friend who has been there in the good times, and the not so good times. He is one who always has a word of wisdom to share, no matter what the situation may be.

One thing I can say about David without hesitation or reservation, is that he is a man who hears God's voice. His past writings have stirred many into a deeper knowledge of what God has for those who are pursuing God with all their hearts. I've seen David's passion for seeking a fresh anointing of the Holy Spirit in his life intensify over the years, not just for himself, but for all who have a desire for freshness too.

In his latest book, **Prophetic Bridges: Discovering God's Pathways To Your Destiny,** David fills the reader with his wisdom and provides spiritual truths for the Body of Christ

David Mayorga

for anyone who is hungering for all that God has for them.

As I read the pages of this book, I find myself being challenged, like many of you will be, to not hold back. Even if at times we might not see what is on the other side of the bridge, it is essential that we cross the bridges to our destiny; so that we may see our God given dreams come to pass.

If you have a God given dream, this book will help you, encourage you, and cause you to keep pressing in to fulfill your dream. Things may seem impossible for you, but they are not impossible for God. The impossible part is God's part, the possible part is yours and mine. Think about this: Anyone can hold up a rod, but only God can part the sea, anyone can roll away a stone, but only God can raise the dead back to life.

May your faith be challenged to cross the bridges in your life that will bring you to your destiny and may everything that God desires to do with you and through you become the passion of your life.

David Mayorga

Discovering God's Pathways to Your Destiny

- Tom Carubba, Senior Pastor
Hosanna World Changers Church, Brownsville, Texas

David Mayorga

Preface

When I think of bridges, I think of pathways that will take me across an area that I am not otherwise able to reach. I believe that there are many bridges in our lives which we must cross at any given time. If we cross, we will advance and see infinite opportunities. If we don't cross, we will never know all that was in store for us.

Now, not all bridges that we are meant to cross are natural. Many of the bridges that a servant of God must cross will be, for the most part, spiritual. As a matter of fact, bridges start off "in the spirit" first, and then manifest in the natural.

My inspiration for writing this manuscript came from the words a prophetic man spoke into my life at a Morningstar Prophetic Conference in Fort Mills, SC in May of 2019.

On the second day of our four-day conference, this older saint of God came up to me and began to prophesy over my life and ministry. My only other previous encounter with this servant was at our lunch table the day before. He and his wife shared with my friend and I, the great things God had been doing through their lengthy ministry.

They both seemed very excited about all that the Lord had done through their lives in the many years of serving God. All I can say, is that they were extremely zealous for God, not to mention how encouraged I was by their devotion and hunger to advance God's kingdom.

As I was waiting for the session to begin, he approached me. These were his words: "The day is coming when you will see bridges appear. When you see them, you will be challenged to cross them. You are not to worry about what you leave behind, for the Lord Himself, will take care of all that you leave behind you. As soon as you cross over, you will enter new opportunities. By this time, the bridge that you cross, will disappear!"

David Mayorga

Prophetic Bridges

As he prophesied to me, I felt my heart burning. I know it was the Lord getting me ready to enter new opportunities for my life and ministry.

Since this Prophetic Conference back in May of 2019, the Lord has kept this prophetic word very close to my heart. I'm not sure where all this is going, but one thing I know for sure, God is able to take me there, if I am willing to go!

The desire to put this whole idea into writing began stirring in my mind right after that specific prophetic word was given to me. It is for this reason, that I felt strongly from the Lord, to reveal this part of His heart to the body of Christ, His church. It is with this pure motive and intent that I have taken on the challenge to hear His voice and prophesy God's heart.

I know that most believers are in constant transition mode. We are always moving God-ward and into our destiny. Most of the challenges we face are the result of us either crossing some bridge of opportunity, or not crossing it.

David Mayorga

Discovering God's Pathways to Your Destiny

We are where we are, because that is where we decided to be!

- David Mayorga, *Executive Director*
Masterbuilder Ministries, Palmhurst, Texas

David Mayorga

Introduction

Bridges: Where Did the Idea Come From?

Before I begin to unfold the spiritual perspective of this writing, I would like to share with you some very important facts regarding the history of bridges.

It is very interesting to find out where the whole idea of a bridge originated, what the process of building one entails, and its purpose. I do believe this information will allow us to make a deeper connection and give us a greater appreciation for the "why" we need spiritual bridges in our lives.

History of Bridges

Let me begin by saying that the topic of bridges and its history is pretty simple but at the same time profound. While the idea of building a bridge may seem somewhat simplistic once mastered, the end result and purpose is what holds the true essence of it all, thus making bridges a remarkable breakthrough in history.

As I began my research, I discovered that stepping-stones were perhaps the earliest method used to cross a pond of water, a river or a creek. Stepping-stones would be set in such a way as to provide a bridge for people to be able to cross over from one place to another.

Even though no one really knows where the idea originated, stepping-stones, along with bridges made out of logs, were the earliest forms for crossing bodies of water. ("Glossary of Trail and Greenway Terms". South Carolina State Trails Program. 2008. Retrieved 5 January 2014).

Along with these types of bridges, the Neolithic people also built a form of boardwalk across marshes, which still exist in England and are approximately 6000 years old. (Brunning, Richard (February 2001). "The Somerset Levels". Current Archaeology. XV (4) (172 (Special issue on Wetlands): 139-143).

David Mayorga

Taking these facts into account, it's safe to say that ancient peoples also used log bridges that fall naturally or are intentionally placed across streams. (National Parks Conference, Department of the Interior (1915). Proceedings of the National parks conference held at Berkeley, California March 11, 12, and 13, 1915. Washington, DC: Government Printing Office. P. 60. Retrieved March 14, 2010).

Now, the greatest bridge builders of the distant past were the ancient Romans. The Romans built arch bridges and aqueducts that could stand in conditions that would damage or destroy earlier designs. Some are still standing today. ("History of Bridges". Historyworld.net. Archived from the original on January 6, 2012. Retrieved January 4, 2012).

In the history of bridges, whether a bridge was built naturally or intentionally, whether it was used for the sake of crossing over to visit a friend or to attack an army in time of war, the purpose of a bridge still remains - to provide a pathway to the other side.

David Mayorga

Discovering God's Pathways to Your Destiny

The Holy Spirit is the Bridge-Maker!

It is my prayer that you were able to get a glimpse of what a bridge is, a bit of its history and how it will make a way for our destinies.
There are many rivers, valleys, mountains and yes, many obstacles yet to cross in our lifetime.

We will be challenged time and time again to cross over a difficult place. If we face these challenges with a receptive heart to His will, we will see the bridges that He brings about in our lives in order to accomplish this.

Open your heart to the Holy Spirit and invite Him to open your understanding while you study these notes.

I do believe that there are some things that man cannot do without the leadership of the Holy Spirit in his life.
Now, if we entrust ourselves unto the Lord for direction, without doubt, I believe that a much-needed bridge will open up

David Mayorga

Prophetic Bridges

for all those who are looking for one. So....

Step into Him!

David Mayorga

Chapter 1

Prophetic Bridges Are More than a Pathway – They Are Opportunities!

I don't claim to be a philosopher of any sort, but an important thing I have come to learn through the years is this: Unless I am willing to take certain risks, I may not see the possibilities.

Taking risks can be a very scary thought. Many have decided to "stay put," while others have plunged into great ventures by taking risks. Many saw great success and many experienced great failures.

Frederick Wilcox sums it up in his quote: *"Progress always involves risks. You can't steal second base and keep your foot on first."*

Risk-Taking!

What does the word risk mean?

Prophetic Bridges

According to Webster's Dictionary, risk means 1: possibility of loss or injury; 2: someone or something that creates or suggests a hazard. To take a risk at anything means then, to take the chance of losing something! Do you see why people are so slow in acting out the challenges that stand before them? Do you see why people are slow at moving with what they feel in their hearts?

Everything that is worth anything, requires first a risk. Risks must be taken so that the "door of opportunity" can open!

Starting a business, or a ministry, applying for a job, learning to swim, joining a basketball team, buying a car, or a home, getting married, starting a family, talking to someone about the love of Jesus Christ, are a few examples of decisions that make us vulnerable to rejection, or some kind of risk. However, one must take a risk if there is ever going to be some type of advancement.

Widowed and Poor!

David Mayorga

Looking up, [Jesus] saw the rich people putting their gifts into the treasury. And He saw also a poor widow putting in two mites (copper coins). **And He said, Truly I say to you, this poor widow has put in more than all of them; For they all gave out of their abundance** (their surplus); **but she has contributed out of her lack and her want, putting in all that she had on which to live."** (Luke 21:1-4)

Here's an interesting story I found as I meditated upon God's Word in regard to laying it all out without reserves, regrets or retreats.

This is the story of a poor widow who Jesus happened to keep His eye on as the time for giving offering at the temple took place. The first thing that Jesus noticed was how the rich were putting their gifts into the treasury and at the same time, a poor widow showed up with her offering.

To everyone's surprise I'm sure, Jesus commended the widow for her offering. He said, **"Truly I say to you, this poor**

widow has put in more than all of them!" Can you imagine everyone thinking and in essence saying, "Jesus, come on! Didn't you see the amount which the rich put in? That poor widow does not even come close to the offering given by the rich!"

Giving Out of Our Surplus

To everyone's amazement, Jesus said, **"For they** [the rich] **all gave out of their abundance** (their surplus)**; but she has contributed out of her lack and her want, putting in all that she had on which to live."**

In God's economy, it is really all about the heart. Jesus was not impressed by the amount given by the rich, not because it was not a good amount; He was moved because their hearts were reserved to give abundantly!

In Jesus' Pocket!

David Mayorga

On the other hand, the widow, "**…contributed out of her lack and her want, putting it all that she had on which to live.**" In other words, Jesus noticed that this woman really had nothing to cling on to, but God. What good was two coins in her possession versus putting those two coins in Jesus' pocket?

The spiritual man will always have a deeper reason for laying his life down. Risk-taking is truly an easy thing to do when you catch a glimpse of where you are headed!

If we were to ask the widow, "Why did you risk in giving everything you had?" She would probably reply something like this: "I gave it all because for two pennies, I get to have free breath, free life, free sunshine, and a great opportunity to tell God that He is my everything!"

Israel Had to Make a Choice!

"**Moses sent them to scout out the land of Canaan, and said to them, Get up this way by the South (the Negeb) and** go up into the hill country, And see what the land is and whether the people who dwell there are strong or weak, few or many, And whether the land they live in is good or bad, and whether the cities they dwell in are camps or strongholds, And what the land is, whether it is fat or lean, whether there is timber on it or not. And be of good courage and bring some of the fruit of the land. Now the time was the time of the first ripe grapes. So they went up and scouted through the land from the Wilderness of Zin to Rehob, to the entrance of Hamath. And then went up into the South (the Negeb) and came to Hebron; and Ahiman, Sheshai, and Talmai [probably three tribes of] the sons of Anak were there. (Hebron was built seven years before Zoan in Egypt.) And they came to the Valley of Eshcol, and cut down from there a branch with one cluster of grapes, and they carried it on a pole between two [of them]; they brought also some pomegranates and figs. That place was called the Valley of Eshcol [cluster] because of the cluster which the Israelites cut down there. And they returned from scouting out the land after forty days. They came to Moses and Aaron and

David Mayorga

to all the Israelite congregation in the Wilderness of Paran at Kadesh, and brought them word, and showed them the land's fruit. They told Moses, we came to the land to which you sent us; surely it flows with milk and honey. This is its fruit. But the people who dwell there are strong, and the cities are fortified and very large; moreover, there we saw the sons of Anak [of great stature and courage]. Amalek dwells in the land of the South (the Negeb); the Hittite, the Jebusite, and the Amorite dwell in the hill country; and the Canaanite dwells by the sea and along by the side of the Jordan [River]. Caleb quieted the people before Moses, and said, let us go up at once and possess it; we are well able to conquer it. But his fellow scouts said, we are not able to go up against the people [of Canaan], for they are stronger than we are. So they brought the Israelites an evil report of the land which they had scouted out, saying, The land through which we went to spy it out is a land that devours its inhabitants. And all the people that we saw in it are men of great stature. There we saw the Nephilim [or giants], the sons of Anak, who come from the giants; and we were in our

David Mayorga

own sight as grasshoppers, and so we were in their sight." (Numbers 13:17-33)

When taking a risk, one must understand that it is truly a way to advance any cause. Risk has always been a thing of faith. Either you believe it in your inner-man, or you don't.

In the story of Israel advancing into the Promised Land, some things were required. To begin with, they were challenged to believe all that God had promised them. Obviously, this was not an easy thing for Israel. They requested spies to be sent out and have the land "checked-out" to see if all that God had said was true about this Promised Land.

As you can imagine, this did not sit well with the Lord. After the spies released their report of their findings, the people of God still rejected the idea of possessing the land God promised to give them. They were not willing to risk their lives, their families and their possessions for something greater. Due to their lack of faith they were paralyzed by what they heard and saw with their very eyes.

The Scripture says that **"without faith, it is impossible to please God."** (Hebrews 11:6) If the element of faith is missing from our lives, then we will end up living "dead-end lives." What is God to do when we won't lend ourselves to follow-through with the directives that He gives us? Israel had to make a choice and they did – they chose not to cross over into their promise! As a consequence, death was their portion.

You and I will be challenged in the same way…

Too Timid, Too Shy, Too Insecure!

I'm not sure if my upbringing had anything to do with my timidity as a young man, but boy, did I have a hard time standing in front of people when I was younger.

In High School when I was asked to do oral reports – I would not do it! I would take a big fat zero as my grade instead. How great was my timidity? My fears? My insecurities? I think back and realize how bound I was as a young man. Yet God was gracious and saw me through.

When I came into the kingdom of God, I remember attending Sunday School. I remember the time when my Sunday School teacher asked me if I would be willing to teach the class the following Sunday because he was going out of town. I was so scared at the thought of standing in front of the class that I had to come up with a lie! I told the Sunday school teacher that I was going out of town too! Can you believe that? I'm sure God has forgiven me for that one.

A Bridge of Opportunity for Me

As I grew in the things of the Lord, I began to understand more and more the value of understanding God's wishes, His desires, His heart, His purpose, etc. Let me share a personal experience of a specific "bridge" that appeared to me back in

1990.

While working at a manufacturing plant, I had already felt the Lord's calling upon my life. My pastor and I had already met for the purpose of sharing my sentiment in wanting to get into full-time ministry and all he said to me was, "Stay in prayer and wait for God's timing!"

One evening after work, my pastor reached out to me and called me at home. He said to me, "David, do you still want to come into full-time ministry?" I had been anticipating this opportunity but never thought it would come in the way it did. "Of course!" I said to him.

This was the beginning of a ride with God that has lasted more than thirty years. Did I know things would turn out like this? Absolutely not!

No Regrets!

David Mayorga

Prophetic Bridges

In retrospect, I am glad things happened the way they did. I am glad that I took the step when I did, how I did it and how it all unfolded for me.

Since taking those steps of faith, I have come to a place in my own life where I believe God had destined me to be. Had I not taken those steps – only God knows of the outcome.

I have learned that opportunities really come when we are looking for them. As your heart makes the request known (whether spoken or an unspoken request,) it will set things in motion for you. It is at this point where bridges and pathways begin to appear before you.

David Mayorga

Chapter 2

Understanding Where You Are Now

I would like to open this chapter by turning our focus to looking at our lives in the light of a bigger picture – the big picture of God for you.

Why Is My Life This Way?

Too often, throughout life's journey, we enter periods of great adversity, the kind that brings about confusion leaving us with an anxious heart. Is this part of God's plan for development? We'll I'm sure there is some smart theologian or psychologist that can try to explain this or give some theory to it, but here is what I have learned: When you walk with God, a breaking process is always in order for the purpose of God's end result in you.

Let us look at this:

The Inward Process

"Most assuredly, I say to you, unless a grain of wheat falls into the ground and dies, it remains alone; but if it dies, it produces much grain." (John 12:24)

One of the things that Jesus taught all of us was this principle: If there is no death to a seed, then there will be no future to it. A seed is the beginning of a new opportunity. If it is planted and falls into the ground, it will germinate and break, producing new life.

You and I must go through the process of breaking if we are to see fruit. There will be no fruit unless death takes its rightful place first.

Once the seed comes forth, there is no telling how much fruit will be produced and multiplied from it – there is just no telling of all that God can do!

David Mayorga

The Inward Experience

"Blessed be the God and Father of our Lord Jesus Christ, the Father of mercies and God of all comfort, who comforts us in all our tribulation, that we may be able to comfort those who are in any trouble, with the comfort with which we ourselves are comforted by God. For as the sufferings of Christ abound in us, so our consolation also abounds through Christ. Now if we are afflicted, it is for your consolation and salvation, which is effective for enduring the same sufferings which we also suffer." (2 Corinthians 1:3-6)

Once we have experienced an "inward breaking," we will reap the benefit of experiencing the comfort of God. There is no other feeling in this world that could compare to it! To have God come by and through His Spirit teach us first-hand about His love, compassion and comfort, has to be the ultimate joy! By the way, this can only be felt after the process of "inward breaking."

David Mayorga

The amazing thing about this experience is not only that we have received comfort and care, but along with that experience, we have also received the foundation for a true expression of His nature. In other words, the foundation to a new ministry has been developed. We are now ready to give what we have, to someone in need.

The Outward Expression

But I want you to know, brethren, that the things which happened to me have actually turned out for the furtherance of the gospel, so that it has become evident to the whole palace guard, and to all the rest, that my chains are in Christ; and most of the brethren in the Lord, having become confident by my chains, are much more bold to speak the word without fear." (Philippians 1:12-14)

Paul said that what had happened to him has actually turned out to be a good thing – to advance the gospel!

David Mayorga

Discovering God's Pathways to Your Destiny

So, what happened to Paul? He was arrested and put away in prison. It was definitely a bridge to cross – but did Paul know that this awaited him? Probably not.

I really don't think being put in a prison really scared him. Paul had already died to self (Galatians 2:20) and was so far away from trying to prove anything to this world. He was ready to die for the sake of Christ as he had previously voiced. Listen: "Now when we heard these things, both we and those from that place pleaded with him not to go up to Jerusalem. Then Paul answered, **"What do you mean by weeping and breaking my heart? For I am ready not only to be bound, but also to die at Jerusalem for the name of the Lord Jesus."** (Acts 21:12, 13)

All the breaking that took place in Paul's life, not only empowered him within, but also gave him courage and a fiery message to go along with that so that the gospel could be advanced everywhere he went!

David Mayorga

Some bridges are not as pretty and as promising as you might think. They may look that way, but as you begin to cross, it might shake you to your very core.

The Good, the Bad and the Ugly!

I am almost sure that many things have transpired in your life. Some things have been great, some things have been exceptionally awesome; yet some things may have been ugly and negative in your life and you wish to forget them.

I have heard people who were in great duress or distress say, "I wish I could forget this part or chapter of my life!" Others have said, "I wish this would have never happened." So, there are many experiences that have contributed to our growth and development – whether good or bad, they have taught us much.

Your Past Can Shed Light

David Mayorga

Discovering God's Pathways to Your Destiny

In spite of all that we have learned so far, there is still so much to "enter into."

In full view of what the past has taught me, to some degree, it gives me revelation of where I am today. One of the things that brings understanding to me is asking myself the question, "Where was I, before the opportunity came?" Was I fulfilled? Was I satisfied with my present state? The answer would probably be "No!"

You see, our past was a place where we had arrived at based on our decisions made prior. So, it is safe to say that we have been on a journey to greater fulfillment in all that God has designed within us.

I can truly say that my past and all the decisions that I have made, affected and are affecting my present state.

Is there more for me? Absolutely!

David Mayorga

Knowing that my heart is God's house, a continual picture of my destiny is ever before me. What I am living out now, is just a result of bridges I have crossed throughout my life.

Your Future Is Wrapped Up in Him!

"For I know the thoughts and plans that I have for you, says the Lord, thoughts and plans for welfare and peace and not for evil, to give you hope in your final outcome." (Jeremiah 29:11 Amplified Version) Because God has given us a hope and future, we are positioned for greatness in Him! No one who trusts the Lord, ever needs to worry about their future ever again!

We can always know for a fact that the Lord Himself will reveal to us His plan; and His plan will always be to bring us into a place where we will be enriched and blessed by Him. Of this, I am confident.

Every pathway, every door or bridge that the Lord will bring us to, will always serve the purpose of bringing us into a greater fullness of His destiny. Our life just gets brighter and brighter as we allow Him to lead us.

Mistakes: Life's Greatest Teacher

Before I leave this chapter, I want to assure you that you are on the right track. Just because things have not quite turned the way you wanted, trust me, you are on the path to greatness.

It is so easy to discard God's will in your life due to circumstances, obstacles and even crucial mistakes. Let me just say a little bit about this…

When we talk about making mistakes in life, we can almost bet that every human being has felt the pain of "missing the mark" at one point or another.

Through the years, I have had the privilege of meeting some

of the finest people around. They are not celebrities, they are not super stars, they are not Nobel Peace Prize winners; they happen to be everyday citizens who venture daily to make "life" happen. All of them are pursuing their dreams the best way they can! To me, this is admirable.

In all this, all of them have made mistakes. Some mistakes were serious and extremely consequential; other mistakes were easy to overcome, while other mistakes have lingered on for years and in some cases, for generations.

Mindset of Bridge-Crossers

As ugly and as painful as a mistake may appear, it is only a matter of time that it will turn into a bridge filled with countless opportunities. The one and only requirement is that one needs to hang on to the mercy of God and trust the Lord with the process.

People who have crossed countless bridges, know all too well

Discovering God's Pathways to Your Destiny

of the process that it entails. In spite of the uncertainty that might fill their hearts, they know for certain that a bridge is about to appear!

You are where you are now because of all that has happened in your life – mistakes included. Don't discard your experiences in life, especially the negative ones! Learn to recognize what has brought you here now.

David Mayorga

Chapter 3

Abraham: A Bridge for the Making of a Nation!

"Now faith is the substance of things hoped for, the evidence of things not seen." (Hebrews 11:1)

In my experience in walking with the Lord, I have come to understand many things pertaining to taking "steps of faith."

Steps of faith are not steps taken in recklessness. No, steps of faith are strategic steps taken in God's direction. It is when one hears the Lord and moves by the Lord's command. This would be a walk of faith.

Now, many people like sensationalism and talk about taking steps of faith even though God has not spoken. It's almost like a "hit and miss." They say, "God told me to do this brother." After a while, you never hear back from them and it leaves you wondering...What ever happened to that "word," that "prophecy?"

The truth is that people didn't move by faith – there was no bridge there! They made their "faith" something of the flesh. It was a mental (in the metaphysical realm.) This happens often. We have too many saying God said this and that, but their fruit shows it wasn't true!

Let me shed some light into what it truly means making God's voice a bridge for us. Without this bridge, it is impossible to cross into God's "desired end" for us. I will show you this truth using several examples from both the Old and New Testament.

Abraham: A Bridge to the Making of a Nation

"Now the LORD had said to Abram:
"Get out of your country,
From your family
And from your father's house,

To a land that I will show you.
I will make you a great nation;
I will bless you
And make your name great;
And you shall be a blessing.
I will bless those who bless you,
And I will curse him who curses you;
And in you all the families of the earth shall be blessed."
So, Abram departed as the LORD had spoken to him..."
(Genesis 12:1-4)

In studying the life of Abraham, I find that Abraham was a man who could hear God. Now, did Abraham know what God would be requesting of him? I think not. This brings us to the idea that God often reveals His intentions to people who are willing to listen to Him.

In the mind and heart of Abraham from what we read, there doesn't seem to be any intention of him moving anywhere. Not to another neighborhood, not to another town, and much less to another nation.

Naturally, most people tend to settle where they are, and perhaps have very little desire to make big changes. And so, all too often, people are content with themselves and make their present situation work for them.
I believe Abraham was pretty content. I believe Abraham had no desire to go anywhere much less take all his belonging to another place. Can you imagine this move and taking all his belongings with him? And for what? And where? And why? And for how long?

Things didn't seem that they would be changing for Abraham and his family until the voice of God came and revealed to Abraham God's intent!

I want you to think about this for a bit.

Why Our Lives Are Comfortable

David Mayorga

Prophetic Bridges

There is really never a desire to go anywhere or do anything that is not on our daily agenda, unless our eyes catch a glimpse of something, or our ears hear a certain sound—then, our interest is awaken. I have seen where our curiosity has been stirred by the supernatural world. The challenge to pursue this "spiritual invitation" if you will, arises within us.

When crossing a bridge, usually we do it when we are driving on some highway crossing an ocean, a mountain range or a deep valley. What I am saying is that we only cross bridges out of need, not because we love to do it.

Our motivation for crossing a bridge is usually not for the experience of crossing a bridge but reaching our place of destination.

In the case of Abraham, motivation came from above. God met Abraham and told him, **"Get out of your country..."**

The bridge came from above, from the voice of Jehovah God.

David Mayorga

Basically, in essence, God told Abraham, "I'm taking you to a place where I will be making a nation out of you. I know you don't know this, but I'm telling you. My words will form a bridge under your feet. You will walk on my words and get to that place I desire and need you to be Abraham. I will take care of all the details, just walk on my words."

I used to wonder why people don't feel motivated to move forward with their lives, with their careers, with their businesses, etc. I believe that, too often, people don't have a bridge to walk on!

God's Intent

As the Lord moves in our lives, very few servants of God are aware of His intent. I do believe that everything God does is intentional. Every word, every action, every little thing that happens to us, is part of, or even key to our alignment in God. To be invited by the Spirit of the Lord to "get out" of our country, is no laughing matter. Actually, what is really happening, is that God is "pushing" His agenda on humanity through you. You should feel honored for such a high calling in God!

Appropriating It by Faith

In building this bridge that God designed for Abraham, it is important for Abraham to make a decision. He must appropriate these words by faith. It is only through the faith of God that motion would take place. You see, earthly ideas usually don't have the power or even the emotion needed to make such jumps of faith.

How many people do you know who said, "God told me to move by faith?" Yet, when they did finally move, things didn't work out. Why not? It wasn't God's faith! It was metaphysical (soulish) faith.

Simple wishing is not going to cut it. Confessing something that God never spoke into your spirit, will not get it done! You can "name and claim" all you want, but you will not see the hand of God!

In closing this narration of Abraham's challenge, one thing I know, one thing I have seen – Once the words of God come forth, you can trust that a bridge has been laid under your feet! God will keep building it as long as you keep walking on it! Isn't this a phenomenal thought?

David Mayorga

Chapter 4

Noah: God's Bridge-Builder for Generations Yet to be Born!

"This is the genealogy of Noah. Noah was a just man, perfect in his generations. Noah walked with God. And Noah begot three sons: Shem, Ham, and Japheth. The earth also was corrupt before God, and the earth was filled with violence. So God looked upon the earth, and indeed it was corrupt; for all flesh had corrupted their way on the earth. And God said to Noah, "The end of all flesh has come before Me, for the earth is filled with violence through them; and behold, I will destroy them with the earth. Make yourself an ark of gopherwood; make rooms in the ark, and cover it inside and outside with pitch. And this is how you shall make it: The length of the ark shall be three hundred cubits, its width fifty cubits, and its height thirty cubits. You shall make a window for the ark, and you shall finish it to a cubit from above; and set the door of the ark in its side. You shall make it with lower, second, and third decks. And behold, I Myself am bringing floodwaters on the earth, to destroy from under heaven all flesh in which is the breath of life; everything that is on the earth shall die. But I will establish My covenant with you; and you shall go into the ark—you, your sons, your wife, and your sons' wives with you. And of every living thing of all flesh you shall bring two of every sort into the ark, to keep them alive with you; they shall be male and female. Of the birds after their kind, of animals after their kind, and of every creeping thing of the earth after its kind, two of every kind will come to you to keep them alive. And you shall take for yourself of all food that is eaten, and you shall gather it to yourself; and it shall be food for you and for them. Thus Noah did; according to all that God commanded him, so he did." (Genesis 6:9-7:1)

As part of the topic: *God's Voice is a Prophetic Bridge for You*, I want to continue pointing out the different ways that God brings us [by forming a bridge,] from one point to another; from one idea into another and so forth.

David Mayorga

Prophetic Bridges

I want to bring you now into a powerful revelation that Noah had during a very crucial time in human history.

Apparently, mankind had truly become very wicked and indifferent towards God. Listen to this: **"The earth also was corrupt before God, and the earth was filled with violence. So God looked upon the earth, and indeed it was corrupt; for all flesh had corrupted their way on the earth."** Based on what we read here, what do you think God was supposed to do with such a mess? The answer might surprise you, and then again, maybe not.

It is obvious to see that God didn't like how man had turned away from Him and followed their own instincts and desires. This brought man into a lifestyle of violence... **"And God said to Noah, "The end of all flesh has come before Me, for the earth is filled with violence through them; and behold, I will destroy them with the earth."** It is a harsh reality to know that God was not happy with the outcome of mankind's approach to living on earth and said to Noah, "...I

David Mayorga

will destroy them with the earth."

Let me add a point of interest here: When man is left to deal with life on his own [his own strength, his own way of thinking, his own way of processing life, and his own will-power,] he will manage to destroy it in no time! Is it any wonder why people are broken and shattered to pieces all around us? Just something to think about.

Moving on...

God Looked for a Man

After God made up His mind on what He was about to do on the earth, He looked for a man who could carry this idea to fruition.

As it usually is with God, He will not do anything without letting His prophets or His servants know what He is about to do on the earth [see Amos 3:7.] He always shares His heart with those who care to listen!

So, the Lord found a man by the name of Noah. Noah was the man God took pleasure in and trusted him fully with this revelation and thus, gave him the bridge to save mankind. This bridge came by direct revelation from the Lord, and God unfolded this whole idea to Noah.

It's God's Blueprint: A "Detailed" Bridge!

"Make yourself an ark of gopherwood; make rooms in the ark, and cover it inside and outside with pitch. And this is how you shall make it: The length of the ark shall be three hundred cubits, its width fifty cubits, and its height thirty cubits. You shall make a window for the ark, and you shall finish it to a cubit from above; and set the door of the ark in its side. You shall make it with lower, second, and third decks. And behold, I Myself am bringing floodwaters on the earth, to destroy from under heaven all flesh in which is the breath of life; everything that is on the earth shall die…"

David Mayorga

Discovering God's Pathways to Your Destiny

One of the most interesting things that God does when sharing His heart, is how He details what He desires to be constructed or built.

In the case of this revelation, the Lord reveals to Noah an ark. God instructs Noah with specifics. He gives Him the materials to use, the size of this unique ark, and exactly what to do after it is completed. Amazing isn't it?

Keep in mind at all times, that if the Lord has a bridge that He needs built, He will always provide the details for it. It is the same way in our daily walk with the Holy Spirit. The Spirit is the mind of God and He will come and reveal all of God's intents and how to accomplish them.

Noah's Attitude: Quick to Hear and Quick to Obey!

"By faith Noah, being divinely warned of things not yet seen, moved with godly fear, prepared an ark for the saving of his household..." (Hebrews 11:7a)

David Mayorga

What is the standpoint that one should take after receiving a revelation from the Lord? Once we hear God, and He shows us a "bridge" to build, what should our attitude be? I mean, should we be diligent with it? Should we be serious about it? How about the urgency of it? Can we afford to mess around and "drag our feet" until kingdom come? By no means!

I believe that the general rule to following instructions from the Lord should always be, quick to hear Him and quick to obey Him!

In the book of Hebrews, the Scripture show us a picture of what it looked like right after Noah got this revelation from the Lord. The Scripture says that Noah, **"...being divinely warned of things not yet seen, moved with godly fear and prepared an ark..."**

Bridge-Making Requires Action!

After Noah hears God, he did two things: he [Noah] moved

with godly fear (this is internal,) and then prepared an ark (this is external.)

The word moved in the Hebrew means that Noah showed proper and fitting respect to God. In other words, Noah didn't ignore, disrespect, dishonor, neglect, or ignore the instruction of the Lord.

He then proceeded to prepare an ark. The word prepared in the Hebrew means "to build by using materials and/or parts."

Ruined for the Ordinary!

You see, once a man is stirred within; once a man gets a glimpse of "the picture" inside his own heart - he will be ruined for an ordinary life. He will never ever be the same again!

Do you think that Noah after God spoke to him about this ark, went back to a normal lifestyle? Do you think he just pretended not hearing or seeing this "picture in his heart?" I think not!

Actually, I know Noah was never the same! After He heard the Lord, the Scripture says, he **"moved with godly fear, [and] prepared an ark!"** May the wisdom written here, impact the generations that are yet to be born! Selah.

David Mayorga

Chapter 5

Joshua:
Making a Bridge to Conquer the Impossible!

"Now Jericho was securely shut up because of the children of Israel; none went out, and none came in. And the LORD said to Joshua: "See! I have given Jericho into your hand, its king, and the mighty men of valor. You shall march around the city, all you men of war; you shall go all around the city once. This you shall do six days. And seven priests shall bear seven trumpets of rams' horns before the ark. But the seventh day you shall march around the city seven times, and the priests shall blow the trumpets. It shall come to pass, when they make a long blast with the ram's horn, and when you hear the sound of the trumpet, that all the people shall shout with a great shout; then the wall of the city will fall down flat." (Joshua 6:1-5)

As the children of Israel started making their way into their

Promised Land, things were not going to be easy; they would have to fight for everything God had promised them. So, their first challenge came as they faced the city of Jericho.

Now the city of Jericho was an ancient city and very well guarded. As the Scripture says, **"Jericho was securely shut up because of the children of Israel; none went out, and none came in."** In the natural this could be a huge undertaking for Israel; as a matter of fact, Israel had no way of getting through and destroying Jericho, unless... unless God stepped in!

It Takes God!

I believe that in most situations where God wants to make His Name known, He will do something extraordinary. He will make something out of nothing; He will call forth those things that are not, as if they were! He has no limitations to what He can do or will do for us!

I can only imagine what was going through Joshua's mind as he approached the city of Jericho. He probably saw the walls and wondered…How in the world would he be able to bring this city down?

The words, **"See! I have given Jericho into your hand, its king, and the mighty men of valor…"** kept ringing in his ear and in his heart. So then, while listening to God's words, Joshua is also looking at the walls. Do you see or understand what I am saying?

A voice of doubt would come in and then the voice of God came rushing in. I believe this conversation in his head went back and forth for some time. Until "instruction" came in; until the revelation to how this whole city would be destroyed.

God begins to instruct Joshua and shows him how this "particular bridge" to conquer the city of Jericho would be built.

Why God Shows Us the "Impossible" First

David Mayorga

Prophetic Bridges

In my walk with the Lord, I have always noticed how it is. God always shows us the "impossible" part to an endeavor first. He makes us look at the difficulty and the challenge of how it will all take place. Why? I believe this happens because God wants us to see how weak and frail we truly are without Him. He wants us to acknowledge that without Him we can't do anything!

Here's one of the secrets that I have learned in walking with God: When we see with our natural eyes the "impossible feat" and we quickly turn to God and say, "How am I supposed to do this with what I have at hand? Lord you know very well that I don't have it in me to do this!" This is when the Lord steps in and releases His mighty power upon us, over us, inside us or wherever His grace is needed to get the "thing" done!

Seeing the "impossibilities" is not shown to us so we can run away from it, give up or just say, "forget it!" No, no, no! He shows us this so we can acknowledge our weakness first,

David Mayorga

and then His strength in us and through us. This is the real test.

The Test!

He tested Phillip with the feeding of the people, just listen: **"Now the Passover, a feast of the Jews, was near. Then Jesus lifted up His eyes, and seeing a great multitude coming toward Him, He said to Philip, "Where shall we buy bread, that these may eat?" But this He said to test him, for He Himself knew what He would do. Philip answered Him, "Two hundred denarii worth of bread is not sufficient for them, that every one of them may have a little."** (John 6:4-7) The amazing thing about God is that He already knows what He is going to do in any situation. He knows exactly how to provoke us into exercising our faith and trust; the Lord knows who to ask and why he is asking that individual in particular.

Apparently, Philip knew how to count. This much we know of this man. When asked to feed the multitudes, he quickly said, we don't have enough! This is the response of the natural man almost always, when confronted with a difficult situation or an adverse circumstance.

God is Spirit

Whatever God speaks to our hearts must be spiritually apprehended. One cannot hear spiritual words and try to "add them up" in the natural. It will not work.

The realm of the Spirit is a different world. God lives there! Unless we elevate ourselves to this realm [the kingdom of heaven,] we will by no means, be able to see, understand, capture, or make any sense of what God's intents really are!

Joshua had to hear God, believe God at face value, and by faith take himself and his army to that place. What place is that? The place of obedience to God's instruction. The fact that he heard instruction from God didn't qualify him; it was the act of obedience to those instructions that brought him the victory.

The bridge will be made and formed when we take steps of obedience to what God is instructing us to do. Always!

Chapter 6

Peter: A Bridge to Cross-Over

In my endeavor to unveil the theme of this title and continue to unfold this book's message, I often asked myself why only some people get to see the miraculous in their lives. Why does it seem as if some who walk with God experience supernatural encounters and others have yet to experience even one?

My one guess would be that, those who see the supernatural more often, do so because God wants for them to recognize His awesome power. What I mean by this is that, some people have been given keys to unlock doors that have consequential effects impacting others outside their immediate circle of influence, while others never see this side of God.

I believe that if God doesn't show us His power, we will never see God's fullness and ability to do above and beyond what we can think or imagine! So the Lord chooses to unveil His power to those who are looking for it.

Now onto Peter . . .

When I think of an important bible character, the name of the Apostle Peter comes to mind. His life is filled with all kinds of extremities.

Peter is one of the disciples that I have read about, who is answering a question or making a comment when nobody is asking him anything. Yet, in all his human folly, Peter was to become one of the greatest disciples Jesus ever schooled. For three years, Peter walked with Jesus and learned the Master's ways.

In some cases, Peter got it; in others, Peter blew it! Doesn't that sound so much like you and I?

When I started to study the life of Peter, I discovered that his life was filled with many bridges. All the bridges that I see in the Scriptures regarding Peter, were very crucial as history was being made by Jesus our Lord.

Without his knowing, Peter was making history and setting forth a pattern of what a true, down- to-earth disciple was supposed to be. His life, exemplifying the good, the bad and the ugly, left amazing lessons for all of us who would follow Jesus in the generations to come.

In the beautiful gospels and in the book of Acts, you and I have been handed down a manual which journals the life and ministry of the Apostle Peter. His obedience, his disobedience, his impatience, his pride, his enduement of power, his preaching and his testimony of the signs and wonders as performed by his shadow alone, are all recorded here and left for our instruction.

Peter's Essential Bridge-Crossings!

David Mayorga

One of the first bridges that I believe Peter crossed was when Jesus asked him to follow His ministry. The Scripture says, **"And Jesus, walking by the Sea of Galilee, saw two brothers, Simon called Peter, and Andrew his brother, casting a net into the sea; for they were fishermen. Then He said to them, "Follow Me, and I will make you fishers of men." They immediately left their nets and followed Him."** (Matthew 4:18)

Following Jesus without knowing who Jesus was at the time, had to be the craziest thing anyone could ever do. How would they even know if Jesus Christ was the Messiah or not? There was no way of finding that out immediately, unless the Spirit of the Lord had prepared Peter's heart beforehand!

Now don't get me wrong, this could be very possible; and I believe that there had to have been some intervention by the Lord in both, the selecting of Christ's disciples and in them responding accordingly.

David Mayorga

1. Crossing the Bridge of Uncertainty!

In all this decision-making, Peter still had to cross the bridge of uncertainty. He couldn't dwell too long thinking if this was what it meant to "follow God." I would venture to say that, there had to have been some moving of God or stirring in Peter's heart regarding this situation.

The only reason that I'm suggesting that there was already some forethought on this, was because right after Jesus extended His invite, the Scripture says, **"They immediately left their nets and followed Him."** (Matthew 4:20) The word immediately in the original Greek means, "without delay or hesitation; with no time intervening."

Peter and his brother Andrew jumped on this opportunity to follow the King of Glory; and as the Scripture declares, they did it without delay or hesitation!

The reason I called this the bridge of uncertainty is because in life, there will be many bridges that will challenge our faith. We will be called to follow blindly, if you will. Not knowing if we are doing the right thing in crossing a bridge will always be the real challenge for the people of faith. Is it the Messiah or not? Can we trust Him with our future? Will He bring us to the other side? These and many more questions will bombard our thinking process as we attempt to make the best decision.

My dear friends, the secret to saying "yes" to Jesus lies in the revelation deep within your heart. Look for it!

2. Crossing a Supernatural Highway!

"Now in the fourth watch of the night Jesus went to them, walking on the sea. And when the disciples saw Him walking on the sea, they were troubled, saying, "It is a ghost!" And they cried out for fear. But immediately Jesus spoke to them, saying, "Be of good cheer! It is I; do not be afraid." And Peter answered Him and said, "Lord, if it is You, com-

Prophetic Bridges

mand me to come to You on the water." So He said, "Come." And when Peter had come down out of the boat, he walked on the water to go to Jesus." (Matthew 14:25-29)

Another challenge that will come upon many of us is the crossing on a supernatural highway. What is a supernatural highway? I call a supernatural highway anything that is defying to human standard or logic and boggles common sense.

These types of bridges don't have a beginning or an end. Actually, these bridges are not even natural – they are totally supernatural. The Lord causes these bridges to appear as you put confidence and faith in His prophetic spoken word! To the degree that you hear and obey in the Spirit, is the degree that it solidifies or hardens under your feet providing a platform to stand upon!

My other question would be, "Why does God allow us to experience supernatural highways in our lives? My answer would be for the obvious: The Lord desires to take us on this

David Mayorga

supernatural highway to not only manifest His glory to the onlookers, but also to expedite His work through His servants.

Will you go through this supernatural highway when it presents itself? The Lord may ask you to cross a similar bridge only to prove to you that He is the Almighty! Will you go when the Lord says to you, "come"?

3. Crossing Bridges that Invite You into a Deeper Realm!

"Now after six days Jesus took Peter, James, and John his brother, led them up on a high mountain by themselves; and He was transfigured before them. His face shone like the sun, and His clothes became as white as the light. And behold, Moses and Elijah appeared to them, talking with Him." (Matthew 17:1-3)

Bridges also may come in ways where the Lord will invite us to come along with Him. Where are we going, or exactly

Prophetic Bridges

where is He taking us, might not be very clear.

Invitations are perhaps some of the most spontaneous ways that God uses to show us extraordinary things.

In the case of the apostle Peter, Jesus invited him and two others to climb a high mountain; it was here where Christ was transfigured before Peter, James and John. The word of God says that Christ was literally transfigured before them and **"His face shone like the sun, and His clothes became as white as the light."** Can you imagine this wonderful sight?

One question comes to mind: Why didn't Jesus just transfigure Himself at the temple, at the foot of the mountain, or even at the house of Martha and Mary? Why didn't Jesus invite a whole crowd to see Him do this powerful and heavenly manifestation? Why did He do this in front of only three of his disciples?

I believe that these kinds of events only happen by invitation,

David Mayorga

and the person who sees the opportunity to enter into something greater, will come to it! Faith will always be rewarded when done with a pure motive!

4. Crossing the Bridges that Challenge Us to Remain Faithful to God!

"Now Simon Peter stood and warmed himself. Therefore they said to him, "You are not also one of His disciples, are you?" He denied it and said, "I am not!" One of the servants of the high priest, a relative of him whose ear Peter cut off, said, "Did I not see you in the garden with Him?" Peter then denied again; and immediately a rooster crowed." (John 18:25-27)

In the walk of faith, one will also encounter bridges to regression. Not only does the Lord provide bridges for us to cross into our destiny but also the enemy provides bridges for us to go back to where we came from. Do you understand what I am saying?

David Mayorga

Oftentimes, the enemy has provided ways for us to turn back. Maybe the testing is too hard! Maybe the decisions that must be made seem impossible to carry out and we are tricked into seeing only the negative side to it and not the positive result.

I believe Peter had this one day coming. I believe it was in the "agenda of hell" to test this man to the core of his spiritual being!

When challenged by those who had seen him hang out with Jesus, being that Christ had been arrested and was awaiting judgment, Peter quickly disconnected himself from being a follower of Jesus and said, **"I don't know Him!"**

Do you see the enemy providing a wide door for Peter to run back to his old life and pretend that all this Jesus "movement" never really happened and went as far as denying his association with Jesus?

Watch out for these bridges of regression!

David Mayorga

5. Crossing Bridges that Transcend Our Preconceived Ideas and Personal Preferences!

"The next day, as they went on their journey and drew near the city, Peter went up on the housetop to pray, about the sixth hour. Then he became very hungry and wanted to eat; but while they made ready, he fell into a trance and saw heaven opened and an object like a great sheet bound at the four corners, descending to him and let down to the earth. In it were all kinds of four-footed animals of the earth, wild beasts, creeping things, and birds of the air. And a voice came to him, "Rise, Peter; kill and eat." But Peter said, "Not so, Lord! For I have never eaten anything common or unclean." And a voice spoke to him again the second time, "What God has cleansed you must not call common." This was done three times. And the object was taken up into heaven again." (Acts 10:9-16)

I think that one of the biggest challenges to face, or one of the hardest bridges to cross over is this one particular bridge – the bridge of preconceived ideas and personal preferences.

When it comes to personal beliefs and preferences, we all have our pet doctrines and how things should be. The ideas can be so solid that nothing or no one can convince us otherwise. This was the case with Peter. It's easy for God to call a man out of the world, but to take the world out of the man, has to be the biggest challenge yet!

Peter being of Jewish descent knew all too well the law of Moses and how God felt about Gentile practices in lifestyle and religion. Obviously, any devout Jew would have no association with Gentiles, for that was the order of God. Yet, God had another thing in mind – to reach the Gentile through his servants and have the message of the kingdom of God preached to them.

For this job, God had handpicked Peter. Now, Peter was about to have his whole religious experience altered by a trance or a vision from God. Often, God will do this with His servants. Knowing very well that His servants sometimes are too smart for their own good or too wise in their own eyes, God has to "put them to sleep" and visits them in the night through dreams, or during the day using open visions or trances.

The whole key to this is to transcend the human ability to process natural thoughts, and speaking directly into the subconsciousness of our minds – the Spirit of God will get the message to us. He will then stir our hearts to action! This is exactly what happened to Peter.

Our preconceived ideas and personal preferences can be a big hindrance to God's will and can make it almost impossible to cross this bridge without the help of God. So, the Lord, in His mercy, will shut our carnal mind down and speak directly to our spirit-man.

Be on the lookout for prophetic dreams and visions.

David Mayorga

Chapter 7

Saul of Tarsus: "Indeed, I Myself Thought..."

"Indeed, I myself thought I must do many things contrary to the name of Jesus of Nazareth. This I also did in Jerusalem, and many of the saints I shut up in prison, having received authority from the chief priests; and when they were put to death, I cast my vote against them. And I punished them often in every synagogue and compelled them to blaspheme; and being exceedingly enraged against them, I persecuted them even to foreign cities. When the name Saul of Tarsus, the man who became the great apostle for God now named Paul, comes to mind, I think of this one particular man who was enraged with the "Way," and was about to destroy the church of Jesus Christ by putting in jail every loyal disciple and follower of Jesus, what led this man this way?" (Acts 26:9-11)

The Wrong Bridge

David Mayorga

Discovering God's Pathways to Your Destiny

While ministering on the streets one cold winter day just outside our church, which was downtown in the city where I was pastoring at the time, I decided to go out and pass out some blankets to the homeless people hanging out in the surroundings of our ministry base.

As I came across this one particular individual, I reached out to him and offered a blanket, being that it was cold outside and he had very little clothing or at least I felt it wasn't enough to cover him and keep him warm from a cold front that had just arrived. To my dismay, the man pushed the blanket away and rejected my gift. He then proceeded to educate me on how the mind of a homeless man thinks, or at least, his.

This man said to me, "Society has robbed me. There are no good people in the world. The government is a big sham! I hate everyone, and to be honest, I don't appreciate you giving me a blanket." The man continued to express his disgust over my outreach and he just wouldn't receive my help or anyone else's, for that matter.

David Mayorga

Prophetic Bridges

After experiencing this type of rejection, I did not want to stay quiet. I proceeded to make my point to him and said, "You are right about a lot of what you say. I'm really sorry that you feel that way about all that you are saying. But let me tell you, there is a way that brings man into freedom and joy. It is through Christ the Lord. Allow Jesus to come in and change the way you see life; you will see what I mean after you receive Him in your heart." He said, "No! Thank You!" I then walked away pretty brokenhearted.

As I walked away with my blanket in hand, I thought to myself how people experience bad things in life and if convinced that the "misfortune" at hand was the end, then that will be the lenses through which they will see life. This is sad. Very sad!

Too many people that claim to walk with God's Spirit still succumb to damning ideologies and philosophies that derail them from God's eternal purpose. They are still walking on "bridges" that were handed to them by society or bad expe-

David Mayorga

riences and not a bridge that was given to them by the Lord!

I Myself Thought

While putting together this chapter and meditating upon this homeless man, my mind brought me to another man who had also experienced something that perverted his understanding of God and of His Christ.

As studied or well-cultured Saul of Tarsus was, he had a perverted view of who God really was. His religion as a practicing Pharisee had poisoned his understanding and perspective of a loving God full of mercy and grace.

Saul of Tarsus couldn't see how Christ was the fulfillment of the Law and how, through Christ alone, a man could enter the kingdom of God. So, because he couldn't understand it, he wanted to reject the idea and kill it!

Here's what Saul of Tarsus now Paul concluded as he stood

before King Agrippa: **"Indeed, I myself thought I must do many things contrary to the name of Jesus of Nazareth."** Let us spend some time looking at this one verse.

Paul said, **"I myself thought."** What does this mean? Well, let us look at it. The word myself in the original language means own initiative; own sake. The word thought in its original meaning means: to suppose v. – to think or believe (something) without being fully settled in mind or opinion.

Paul within himself and by his own initiative and for his own sake, supposed that he was doing the right thing. Arresting God's servants was normal to his way of thinking. Paul crossed a bridge that was founded on his own ideology. It wasn't birthed in God's Spirit – it was birthed in flesh!

Have you ever made decisions based on assumptions? Have you ever followed a road that you thought or that someone told you, "This is the way?" Only to realize that this direction taken based on assumptions has led you to a dead-end. Or maybe not where you expected to be.

I can only think of how often I, myself, have made these suppositions; how many times I had "jumped the gun" and made one mistake after another – all based on an idea that was led by my own initiative and for my own sake.

Prayer Is Required

My understanding to all this is a simple one: one bridge might take you and I into a good path full of prosperity and blessing and another bridge might take us out of the will of God. Our call for all who have Jesus as Lord and the Holy Spirit as our Teacher, is to ask God which is the way we should go.

Allowing God to lead us by His Spirit must be our most heartfelt desire. This should be our heart-cry. We should always make every effort and attempt to be on the bridge God has prepared for us. Let us never be content with anything less than God's perfect bridge for our lives today!

David Mayorga

Chapter 8

John the Revelator: A Bridge to the Future!

"After these things I looked, and behold, a door standing open in heaven. And the first voice which I heard was like a trumpet speaking with me, saying, "Come up here, and I will show you things which must take place after this." Immediately I was in the Spirit; and behold, a throne set in heaven, and One sat on the throne." (Revelation 4:1, 2)

A Door Open in Heaven

If there is one outstanding thing about coming into God's kingdom is the awesome ability to live in two realms simultaneously. You can minister to the world and at the same time see the Lord face to face! How does this sit with you? Can you fathom this?

We as believers live in two dimensions. If you didn't know

this, it's about time someone told you. There is no one who has the ability to do this but only those who walk with God and see God on a daily basis. We can see what the world is saying and at the same time know what God is saying. We can act as Jesus did, or we can imitate the world, if we like. You and I are living testimonies of the glory of God on earth.

As you walk on the earth among God's creation, you will find that some still don't have the revelation of Jesus and have not accepted Him in their hearts. Therefore, there is no Holy Spirit in their lives and much less the wisdom to understand God's plan in its entirety.

For those who spend time in the secret place of prayer with God, many bridges appear. Bridges that will take them from one point to the next. This has to be one of the most exciting elements about being a servant of the Lord – to know Him and to know His plan for your life.

Immediately I was in the Spirit

When John was taken up, he saw a door that was open. This is a door or a portal in the realm of God. The Scripture says that immediately he was "in the Spirit." John was taken into a supernatural dimension where the Spirit of the Lord said to him, **"I will show you things which must take place after this."**

You and I are not exempt from these experiences; we too can experience visions from the Lord. Those who know the Lord, can avail themselves of the dimension of the Spirit and see all that the Lord has drawn up for the future.

Prophetic Bridges

"Moreover the word of the LORD came to Jeremiah a second time, while he was still shut up in the court of the prison, saying, "Thus says the LORD who made it, the LORD who formed it to establish it (the LORD is His name): 'Call to Me, and I will answer you, and show you great and mighty things, which you do not know." (Jeremiah 33:1-3)

David Mayorga

Have you ever been in a difficult situation which you simply see no way out of? No matter how much you screamed, cried and begged – things were not changing by the outburst of emotion? I'm talking about those moments where no amount of pleading was helping and no one around you was cheering you on! Have you been there? Jeremiah was there and countless others have been to this place.

While Jeremiah was still shut up in the court of the prison, the word of the Lord came to him and said, **"Call to Me, and I will answer you, and show you great and mighty things, which you do not know."** Do you see this? When there is no bridge to cross you over – you call upon the Lord to show you one!

There is no problem too big, no situation too difficult, no adversity too strong where the Lord Himself will not provide a bridge for us. One must learn to call upon the Lord if he is to see a way out of any situation. Once a man sets his heart to seek the Lord, the Lord will appear with a bridge of revelation

David Mayorga

to take him to the other side.

The Secret to Overcoming Uncertainty!

"I, John, both your brother and companion in the tribulation and kingdom and patience of Jesus Christ, was on the island that is called Patmos for the word of God and for the testimony of Jesus Christ. I was in the Spirit on the Lord's Day, and I heard behind me a loud voice, as of a trumpet, saying, "I am the Alpha and the Omega, the First and the Last," and, "What you see, write in a book and send it to the seven churches which are in Asia: to Ephesus, to Smyrna, to Pergamos, to Thyatira, to Sardis, to Philadelphia, and to Laodicea." (Revelation 1:9-11)

As I study the theme of bridges for this manuscript, I have come to the realization that the will of God is not trapped by any means. There is nothing that can hinder the plans of the Lord, His future vision of the world or His eternal church.

David Mayorga

By this time in history, the Apostle John is in prison at the island of Patmos. There is a couple of observations that I want to make before closing this chapter.

The first observation has to do with John himself. Before this revelation came to John, what was his state of mind? What was he thinking? Do you think that John was just waiting for his days to be over and close his life with a bang; a life that gave testimony to John's perseverance in Christ and nothing more? Do you think that maybe John was pondering his present condition and feeling sorry for himself that he was in jail and couldn't help the church advance forward? This might have been the case and we will never really know.

Here's what we know...

As John was in jail at the island of Patmos as the Scripture says, **"I was in the Spirit on the Lord's Day, and I heard behind me a loud voice, as of a trumpet, saying, "I am the Alpha and the Omega, the First and the Last,"** and, **"What you see, write in a book and send it to the seven churches which are in Asia: to Ephesus, to Smyrna, to Pergamos, to Thyatira, to Sardis, to Philadelphia, and to Laodicea."** Just when he might have thought that his life was about over, he heard a loud voice behind him, as of a trumpet! Just when the future looked grim – the Lord came in with a mighty bridge! A bridge into the future for the churches in Asia Minor!

What About You and Me?

The second observation I have relates to you and me. Are you thinking that your life is no longer vibrant? Do you think that your "good" days are behind you? Have you wondered if God does have a special mission for you? Do you ever wonder if the Lord will ever use you to make a significant impact in the world you live in today?

It is easy to feel worthless and insignificant; it is easy to feel that your life doesn't really matter for much. I have been at this place way too often to know that it is not over! The Lord

David Mayorga

is not done with anyone or anything that has breath in it. I believe the Lord continues to plan out our futures and forever is aligning our hearts with His.

I believe the Apostle John was up in age (from what tradition says,) and perhaps felt like his life was about to come to a close; but little did he know that God had something more for him. It is the same way with you and me. Keep seeking for God's significant bridges in the seasons to come in your life. There's more there than you know.

David Mayorga

Chapter 9

Invitations, Methods and What Is Left Behind!

As I continue to share with you the value of bridges, and how important they are to the fulfillment of our destiny, keep in mind that bridges may come to us in many different ways. Failing to recognize these bridges may have adverse effects in our lives and end up hurting us in the long run.

In this chapter, I outline my personal experience and the valuable, life-changing lesson I learned with one of the most meaningful bridges I have encountered and crossed in my own life.

Invitations

The invitation to cross a bridge usually comes in many different ways. It all depends upon your present situation, and how the Spirit of the Lord desires to lead.

Discovering God's Pathways to Your Destiny

As I stated earlier, bridges come in different ways. These invitations may come in the form of people, ideas, revelations from the Lord, opportunities, or challenges in both, vocation and personal life. These bridges sometimes come in the midst of adversity, or perhaps a wrong that was committed against us!

For some strange reason, Christians have always taken the stand that if a thing is "negative" in nature, it must be demonic or at least not coming from the Lord. The same goes for the "positive" things in life. If all is going well, we assume that it is God leading us in the way everlasting!

My dear friends, whether it is a positive or negative experience that comes our way, do not be fooled; a servant of the Lord must always allow the test to come and embrace whatever comes their way. While dealing with the challenge, one must ask the Lord about such test, and why it has come, or for what reason it has been brought upon us.

David Mayorga

It is after this that one gets the wisdom to know what to do with such a test or affliction.

Methods

I remember very clearly an experience I had regarding a particular bridge in my life that I knew I would be crossing, I just did not know when.

When this bridge presented itself, it was in the form of a dream. The Lord revealed to me that the governmental structure of my place of employment would be making changes, and that my life would be severely affected by it.

When the dream came to me – I asked the Lord for wisdom and knowledge. I prayed for clarity, and clarity He gave me. The Lord told me that the dream was for me, that it was for my life and ministry. He showed me that it would come, and for me to remain humble at all times.

David Mayorga

Discovering God's Pathways to Your Destiny

These were my thoughts as I pondered the dream:

- Should I put my trust in a dream?
- Should I trust my whole future on this one dream?
- What if the dream was the result of too much pizza for dinner the previous night?
- There is too much at stake (time, money and re sources, etc.) Should I even "toy" with the idea that it is God leading?
- What would people think of me if I cross this bridge?
- How big is the loss if this bridge (thing) doesn't fly?

In our attempt to please God, one needs to know that His Spirit always goes before us. He leads us with clarity and affirmation accompanied by deep subtle peace. This is how you know that you are to cross no matter what your natural eyes see and no matter what your natural surroundings are saying to you.

All crossings of a bridge must be made by having the faith of

David Mayorga

Prophetic Bridges

God!

What to Do with What is Left Behind!

While at the conference in Fort Mills, SC, the man who prophesied to me regarding this particular theme and subject that I am writing about now, the Lord, through His servant, said to me, "Don't worry about what you are leaving behind as you cross the bridges that will appear. I will take care of everything you leave behind."

What does this mean? Does it mean that one crosses without thinking of the people he may hurt by leaving them behind? Does it mean that one should not worry about the financial obligations that one will be leaving behind? Does it mean that one should not worry about the established networks and connections with those of like faith?

What exactly is it, that I am not to worry about?

David Mayorga

A Different Mindset

To this, I felt the Lord directing me to a different dimension of thinking. It did not mean that I was not to worry about all these obligations - it had to do with a higher level of understanding in the will of God for my life.

We have to remember that when the Scripture says in 1 John 4:18 that **"There is no fear in love, but perfect love casts out fear; for fear has torment, and he that fears has not been made perfect in love."** We have to acknowledge that, when the Spirit of God is leading us by revelation to a certain point of crossing a bridge in our lives, we are not to fear. This means the Lord has our backs and we will flourish because of this move. Fear is NOT of the Lord!

If we fear, then faith is not present, and the Lord is not leading. Anything that is not of faith is sin.

This may explain why our lives don't advance much as we

endeavor to make our way into our destiny. God has it all laid out; we just need to follow His leadership.

Heart-Attitudes for Crossing Bridges

There are some key attitudes that I would love for you to embrace as you cross over into God's plan for you and leave behind yesterday's accomplishments. When I say this, I am also very aware that crossing any type of spiritual bridge in life is definitely not an easy thing to do.

Let me share with you what I discovered in Luke 9:

Now it happened as they journeyed on the road, that someone said to Him, **"Lord, I will follow You wherever You go." And Jesus said to him, "Foxes have holes and birds of the air have nests, but the Son of Man has nowhere to lay His head." Then He said to another, "Follow Me."** But he said, **"Lord, let me first go and bury my father." Jesus said to him, "Let the dead bury their own dead, but you go and preach**

David Mayorga

the kingdom of God." And another also said, "Lord, I will follow You, but let me first go and bid them farewell who are at my house." But Jesus said to him, "No one, having put his hand to the plow, and looking back, is fit for the kingdom of God." (Luke 9:57-62)

A person who longs to walk in the will of God and cross bridges that will get them to that place of alignment, must deal with three elements. Here they are…

1. The Element of Security

"I will follow You wherever You go." And Jesus said to him, "Foxes have holes and birds of the air have nests, but the Son of Man has nowhere to lay His head."

When crossing a bridge that God has provided and knowing very well that God has this planned-out for us to take as a challenge, understand that there is no promise of comfort in any way, shape, or form. To think that things will turn out better for us in the immediate future, is to buy into something God never promised. Obviously, God will take care of us, but not until He is done dealing with our carnality. He will deal with our comfort and security. Nothing is secure in life, except for the Lord Jesus and what He presents to us as opportunities. Nothing is more secure in this life than abiding in the center of God's will!

2. The Element of Putting God First

"Then He said to another, "Follow Me." But he said, "Lord, let me first go and bury my father." Jesus said to him, "Let the dead bury their own dead, but you go and preach the kingdom of God."

To this one in particular, Jesus reached out. He said to him, **"Follow Me."** Please notice here that if the Lord is releasing an invitation to us – understand that it is for the purpose of advancement. Now for the challenge at hand, this one individual said, **"Lord, let me first go and bury my father."** The key word in this sentence is first. This man was asking Jesus to please give him time to take care of a personal matter. Jesus said, **"Let the dead bury their dead..."** Do you see this? Was He insensitive? Nothing against family dying and needing to be buried, but Jesus was not going to allow anyone to put something else before Him. In crossing a bridge, God expects us to die to personal preferences and pick up His cause first. Jesus must have the preeminence in all things. When we cross a bridge, we can't be thinking of all that we need to take care of from our past. When we cross a bridge, we put what we have before us first – not what we leave behind! This truth has to do with giving Jesus first place in our lives, no matter what!

3. *The Element of Convenience*

"And another also said, "Lord, I will follow You, but let me first go and bid them farewell who are at my house." But Jesus said to him, "No one, having put his hand to the plow, and looking back, is fit for the kingdom of God."

David Mayorga

Prophetic Bridges

When God gives us a bridge to cross, we can't make it about convenience. Convenience has no place for those who tend to pursue the will of God. What is convenience? Webster's Dictionary has it as freedom from discomfort; ease.

When it comes to taking a step forward in God's direction, one can't afford to pick and choose what they want. They must press into God's wishes, no matter how much discomfort it may bring. One must deal with their emotions before taking any step towards God's will. Unless one is willing to pay the price for crossing that bridge, he or she will have the hardest time dealing with what is left behind.

David Mayorga

Chapter 10

It's Now or Never!

"Then Moses stretched out his hand over the sea; and the LORD caused the sea to go back by a strong east wind all that night, and made the sea into dry land, and the waters were divided. So the children of Israel went into the midst of the sea on the dry ground, and the waters were a wall to them on their right hand and on their left. And the Egyptians pursued and went after them into the midst of the sea, all Pharaoh's horses, his chariots, and his horsemen." (Exodus 14:21-23)

As I bring this manuscript to a close, I would like to make reference to this powerful testimony of how Israel crossed the Red Sea when pursued by Pharaoh and his army.

Can you see how God always moves things according to His will and not our own? God made a promise to the children of Abraham, Isaac, and Jacob, and was not about to abandon them, not even for a minute.

It's amazing what a little pressure can do to our lives when applied personally. Many people don't realize that many times, the Lord Himself has been waiting for us to make a move in His direction. But, due to fears, insecurities, inconveniences, and the like, we never make the move. Do you know what I mean?

In studying this particular chapter in the book of Exodus, I realized a few things about taking a step forward into God's destiny. You see, the Lord had promised the Hebrew children blessing upon blessing in a land that flowed with milk and honey. To see this land, the Hebrew children would have to experience discomfort first, then the blessing. This is usually God's order.

So, what does God begin to do? He begins to cause a crisis in the lives of the Hebrew children. Pharaoh is no longer favoring the Hebrew children and everything sweet began to turn sour. The Hebrew children began to be abused by the slave-drivers of Pharaoh's camp, and this made them cry out to God for deliverance. In response to their pleas, God raised a man by the name of Moses.

It was Moses that delivered the Hebrew children and brought them out of Egypt by the mighty hand of God, doing signs and wonders. It was the plague of the killing of the firstborn that finally made Pharaoh release the Hebrew children from his bondage and set them free.

As they made their way out of Egypt, they came to the banks of the Red Sea. Talk about overcoming the impossible!

It was here that the bridge of God appeared to them when God told Moses to part the Red Sea, **"Then Moses stretched out his hand over the sea; and the LORD caused the sea to go back by a strong east wind all that night, and made the sea into dry land, and the waters were divided."** (Exodus

14:21)

Can you picture yourself with all these two and a half million Hebrew children at the brink of a chaotic collapse? They are all scared with the army of Pharaoh in hot pursuit and the Red Sea before them. What would you have done?

One thing I have come to realize over the years, is that this life is not forever. We have been given a time under the sun to accomplish God's purpose. If we don't learn to recognize the bridges that God has intentionally prepared for us, – we just might miss out on fulfilling God's purpose for good!

The Enemy Will Pursue to the End!

"And the Egyptians pursued and went after them into the midst of the sea, all Pharaoh's horses, his chariots, and his horsemen." (Exodus 14:23)

Because God's prophetic bridges hold so much value for our

spiritual fulfillment, the enemy will not relent. On the contrary, the enemy will continue to pursue us, even when we're about to reach the other side of a bridge. We can always distinguish what kind of impact our crossing will have by what we feel before we cross, while we are crossing, and after we have crossed!

The Egyptians "pursued and went after them into the midst of the sea, all Pharaoh's horses, his chariots and his horsemen." There is a real bona fide reason why the enemy doesn't want God's servants to cross any bridge. The enemy knows all too well that the purpose of crossing a prophetic bridge, is to get closer to the very heart of God and to our destiny in Him.

Is there any wonder why we experience fear in crossing over? The simple idea or thought of leaving someone or something behind plays a number of mixed emotions in our minds. Should I cross? Should I not cross?

It's Now or Never!

David Mayorga

Prophetic Bridges

In closing this manuscript, I want to leave you with the assurance that you and I will always have the choice to follow God's nudging at our spirit thru prophetic bridges. God has always granted us the power to choose the way we should go. Many prophetic bridges will appear before us throughout our lifetime – what we do with them is solely up to us.

May the Spirit of the Lord quicken our mortal bodies to walk in the dimension of God. May we also see every bridge of opportunity that God presents to us, so that we may seize the moment.

My friends, time is of the essence! He that has an ear let him hear what the Spirit is saying. Live with an urgent heart - it is truly now or never!

David Mayorga

Ministry Information

For more information regarding the ministry of Masterbuilder Ministries, Inc., preaching engagements, leadership training or conferences, School of Ministry - feel free to email David Mayorga:

david_mayorga@sbcglobal.net
mayorga1126@gmail.com

Also, check out our website at:
www.masterbuildertx.com

Our ministry can be located at:

Masterbuilder Ministreis, Inc.
3833 N. Tauylro Rd.
Palmmhurst, Texas 78573

David Mayorga

Ministry Resources

The Few
by David Mayorga
A Call to the Road Less Traveled-
The Call to Intimacy with God
ISBN *978-0-9991710-0-4*

Inextinguishable!
by David Mayorga
ISBN *978-0-9991710-8-0*

The Value of the Elements
by David Mayorga
ISBN *978-0-999171-0-4*

David Mayorga

Discovering God's Pathways to Your Destiny

ALL BOOKS CAN BE
PURCHASED THROUGH

SHABAR PUBLICATIONS

www.shabarpublications.com

David Mayorga

www.ingramcontent.com/pod-product-compliance
Lightning Source LLC
Chambersburg PA
CBHW071005080526
44587CB00015B/2354